LIVING BETWEEN
Faith & Fear

NATASHA AUGHTRY

ISBN 978-1-64140-032-9 (paperback)
ISBN 978-1-64140-033-6 (digital)

Christian Faith Publishing, Inc.
832 Park Avenue
Meadville, PA 16335
www.christianfaithpublishing.com

Printed in the United States of America

Before we get started, let's take a moment and define the words *fear* and *faith*.

Fear—a distressing emotion aroused by impending danger, evil, pain, etc., whether the threat is real or imagined; the feeling or condition of being afraid.

Here are a few other words that describe fear as well: apprehension, dismay, dread, terror, fright, panic and horror.

Faith—complete trust or confidence in someone or something.

Here are a few other words that describe the word faith: trust, belief, confidence, conviction, optimism, hopefulness, hope.

So just by briefly glancing at the definitions of our key words— faith and fear—the very first thing that stands out is that the words describing fear include pain, dread, and most importantly is in complete contrast to what God desires for our lives to be.

Fear and faith are total opposites. Fear remains on one end and faith on the other.

Below is a list of fears that people can face or struggle with.

As you read through the list, if you see a fear noted that you currently fight against, begin to start praying over that area, believing God will bring victory and cause you to triumph in that area.

You'll find that as you search God's word out for the fears that plague you, faith will start to grow and this will make you stronger than what is fighting against you.

Various Fears

1. Fear of failure (failing in life, not meeting desired goals, and etc.)
2. Fear of harm or danger (being attacked, raped, being victimized)
3. Fear of rejection (not being accepted, not loved or unwanted)
4. Fear of death (untimely death, dying too soon)
5. Fear of divorce (broken marriages)
6. Fear of health failing (illnesses in the body)
7. Fear of broken relationships (family, friendships, business connections, and etc.)
8. Fear of miscarriage (loss of child in the womb)
9. Fear of generational curses (being overtaken by issues family has fought against, repeating parents, grandparents, and great grandparent's mistakes)
10. Fear of financial loss (worried about lack of money or resources)
11. Fear of loneliness (fear of being alone, being by one's self)
12. Fear of addiction (drugs, sexual additions, alcohol, food, and etc.)
13. Fear of mental breakdown (nervous breakdowns, overwhelmed with life)
14. Fear of heartbreak (fear that a relationship fails, someone breaks your trust, or that things will not work out in a relationship)

15. Fear of broken home or family (family falling apart, split in household, loss of love in a home)
16. Fear of the opinions of other's (overly concerned of how other's see or view your life)
17. Fear of trusting others (mistrust of others because of past hurts or pains)
18. Fear of shame (feelings of humiliation, embarrassment or disgrace because of wrong choices or painful situations one had to face. Blame placed on a person for uncontrollable situations endured)
19. Fear of excelling (being the best or having success)
20. Fear of bad news (expecting bad news, dreading phone calls, or constantly thinking bad news will be told to you)

This list can really go on and on. The beauty is that God is a healer and is able to cause us to rise above all fears that attempt to plague our lives and bring us to ruin.

Below is a verse that I have come to love, and it rings true.

First John 4:18 says, "There is no fear in love; perfect love casteth out fear: because fear has torment.

(Now there is a little more to this verse, but let's just focus on the first part of it.)

It states that there is no fear in love. Fear involves torment and dread.

So when fear comes knocking at the door of your heart, begin stating God's word over that area.

"There is *no* fear in love; perfect love casteth out fear: because fear has torment."

The bottom line is that God's love is perfect. Perfect meaning there is nothing missing or lacking in that love. First John 4:8 declares that God is love.

The next powerful part of 1 John 4:18 is that "perfect love casteth out fear."

So if the love of God is perfect and unflawed, then that love can drive out fear.

A powerful confession that you can begin to say daily is "God's love is perfect and it drives out every fear that I face."

When fear of any kind rises up, try making this confession a part of your day.

The word of God is very powerful, and limitless victories happen when we begin to apply it to our lives.

We will continue to break down and define our key words as we proceed, but first let's look at when fear was first introduced in the word of God.

Genesis 3:7–10 says, "And the eyes of them both were opened, and they knew that they were naked; and they sewed fig leaves together, and made themselves aprons. And they heard the voice of the lord God walking in the garden in the cool of the day: and Adam and his wife hid themselves from the presence of the Lord God amongst the trees of the garden. And the Lord God called unto Adam, and said unto him, Where art thou? And he said, I heard thy voice in the garden, and I was afraid, because I was naked; and I hid myself."

Here we find ourselves right in the beginning—the Garden of Eden.

This is where God created and formed the world with his very spoken words.

Lastly, we find the first man Adam being formed out of the dust of the ground. God breathed into his nostrils the breath of life, and man became a living soul. Adam was placed in the Garden of Eden to dress it and to keep it.

Adam was given clear and concise instructions about the tree of knowledge of good and evil as well as the damaging effects it would have.

Genesis 3:17 says, "But of the tree of the knowledge of good and evil, thou shalt not eat of it: for in the day that thou eatest thereof thou shalt surely die."

Because Adam and Eve knew what was required and asked of them by God, doing contrary to what was asked was wrong and out of order.

So the first note here is that when we step out of the format or blueprint that has been set by God, fear is not far behind.

Even for children, when they're told not to do something and they turn and do it anyway, fear quickly rises.

Conviction soon follows and releases concern along with worry in the heart of that child.

So the next step naturally is that the child feels the need to hide or cover up what was done to avoid correction.

I can remember a few times specifically as a child when I did something wrong and felt the great need to hide what I had done in the hopes of not being found out.

I also remember feeling shame once the wrong was found out as well.

So fears bring shame on the scene. Fear and shame go hand in hand.

Adam and Eve did what they're told not to do, and thus, we see fear coming on the scene. This is the first instance of fear.

Now keep in mind our definition of the word *fear*. Adam and Eve felt all those things the moment they hid from the presence of God.

Genesis 3:10 says, "And he said, I heard thy voice in the garden, and I was afraid, because I was naked; and I hid myself."

Here we see that fear causes them to hide from the one who loved them most and only wanted the best for them.

Fear caused them hide and to flee the place and position that was strategically designed for them.

How many times do we allow fear to make us flee from God's very best that is set up for our lives?

Oftentimes, God's very best for our lives is forfeited because we are in a fleeing position and not a stand-and-trusting position.

Sin causes us to run, hide, and take cover.

Although that sounds silly, it is exactly what occurs each time we step out of the God-given design and structure for our lives.

This very next verse in Genesis 3 is mind-blowing: "And he said, who told thee that thou wast naked?" (Gen. 3:11).

We will stop there and look deeper at this verse.

God begins by saying, "Who told thee that thou wast naked?"

He was saying, "Wait. That is out of the format or blueprint that I designed for you."

"Who told you this?" Meaning who have you been listening or giving your ear to that is speaking contrary to my spoken word over you?

Many times, we step out of the predesigned format that God has for our lives when we allow others to speak into our ears, heart, or spirit.

Proverbs 4:23 says, "Keep thy heart with all diligence; for out of it are the issues of life."

We must safeguard our ears, hearts, and spirit to avoid taking on identities, concepts, or lifestyles that are directly in contrast to what God wants for us.

The bottom line is that anything contrary to God's spoken word is detrimental to our purposes and destinies.

So as God asks Adam and Eve this question, take a moment and ask yourself this same question.

What has caused you to hide or live beneath the desire of God in your life? Are you in hiding?

Who told you that you were naked?

To be naked is to be uncovered or exposed. Sin leaves us in that position, uncovered and greatly exposed to the consequences of sin.

Sin puts us in a position of shame, and the end result is fear.

We are exposed and left wide open to Satan's assaults.

Out of all that God had given Adam and Eve in the garden, all that remained in the end was fear—a fear that cripples, a fear that ties up years, days, and moments of one's life.

You see, even though we don't like to admit it, there is power in fear.

There is a strength in fear that can only be combated by the word of God.

Just as faith has the power to move mountains in your life, fear also has power to cripple and paralyze by placing people in a holding position that interrupts purpose and destiny.

Although Adam and Eve were in a place of wholeness, complete peace, and tranquility, obedience was still required.

Even though God freely gives us all that we have need of, he still requires that we walk within the statutes of his word.

Stepping out of the safety net God has prepared causes issues that we often can't see the full degree of.

The moment the decision was made to go contrary to the word of God, Eve could not see the fruits of her decision.

Adam couldn't see the other side of the choice to take and eat of the fruit.

He couldn't see that he would cause man to have to work the land as Eve was not able to see how childbirth would be affected.

Every decision we make has consequences. Every decision causes a harvest that will come forth in our lives.

The harvest that Adam and Even yielded was an endless pattern of sin, shame, and fear.

The last few moments in the Garden of Eden were not the most memorable moments for Adam and Eve.

The last moment of true uninterrupted peace and calmness was in the Garden of Eden.

The last full moment of complete rest and trust, knowing that all their needs were met and taken care of, was in the Garden of Eden.

The last moment of wholeness where nothing was missing nor broken was found in the Garden of Eden.

The very last moment where there was no fear or worry, just a freedom that solely comes from the presence of God, was also in the Garden of Eden.

Sometimes, you have to stop and remember the moments before great change hit your life.

Looking back in your mind on the way you were and the way you lived prior to fear taking over.

Remember how free you were? Remember how worry was not a part of your day-to-day task?

Take note to go back down memory lane.

I often wonder if Adam and Eve ever walked down memory lane together and truly realized what was forfeited by one choice.

Did they lie awake and think of how they could have done things differently?

Did they ever stop and think about how good they really had it?

You see, it only takes one decision and one choice to utterly change your life.

Thanks be to God that he stands as our advocate and goes the distance to place us back on a path of victory.

First John 2:1 says it plainly: "And if any man sin, we have an advocate with the Father, Jesus Christ the righteous."

So if you currently find yourself driven and controlled by fear, there is hope and that hope is Jesus.

Know that God is your advocate. He will stand and represent you, even when all of hell's wrath is raging against you.

He will stand up for you when the enemy of your soul demands death for your actions.

He will fight for you when shame comes to steal your joy and peace.

He will guard you from guilt and despair if/as they try to wrap themselves around you as a garment.

He works as our banner and goes before us when it seems everything is set up against us.

He is your advocate, and guess what, you never have to beg him to take your case.

He is willing and able to work for you.

As you acknowledge him and his word, he will begin to stand for you.

He is also our judge.

Isaiah 33:22 says, "For the Lord is our judge, and the Lord is our lawgiver; and the Lord is our king, and it is he who will save us."

Let's continue forward as we break down and uncover the true motives of fear.

CONSEQUENCES OF A CHOICE

Looking at the choice that was made by Adam and Eve to eat of the fruit, it resulted in a ripple effect that would pierce the hearts of mankind.

This was a consuming fear that gained control of every person born from that point on.

If you were aware that your next choice or decision had the ability to change the course of many people, would you be a little more careful in your next move?

The moment she was tempted to partake of the fruit, I would have to believe that Eve did not consider the effects that would follow. That's just it—sin is selfish and very self-centered.

Sin deals with the current moment and doesn't focus on the effects that will follow.

The balance weights of the viewpoint of sin are off and can't judge from a clear mind-set.

Let's check out how often the concern of others is mentioned in Genesis 3:4: "And the serpent said unto the woman, Ye shall not surely die: For God doth know that in the day ye eat thereof, then your eyes shall be opened, and ye shall be as gods, knowing good and evil."

Here, there is only focus on Eve and Adam, not on the others who would follow.

As earlier stated, sin is always self-seeking.

It has the highest focus on self-gratification.

I often say it like this: Sin always has *I* in the middle. What can *I* get from this? How can *I* benefit here?

Sadly, there is no true fulfillment that is birthed from sin; it only takes you deeper and farther from the purpose God desired.

James 1:15 says, "Then when lust has conceived, it bringest forth sin: and sin when it is finished, bringest forth death."

So here we see a pattern: lust, sin, and lastly, death.

No matter who you are, if you participate in the pattern of sin in any stage or area, the end result will still be the same without the intervention of God—death.

Romans 5:14 says, "Nevertheless death reigned from Adam to Moses even over them that had not sinned after the similitude of Adam's transgression, who is the figure of him that was to come."

So we see that because of one choice, one decision caused sin to reign and fill the earth.

Because of this, we know that the course of the world had shifted away from the pattern that God originally designed for mankind.

A shift from the consistent peace that God longed to rule in the hearts of mankind.

Sin causes us to shift from the heartbeat of God. Sin pushes and pulls us from our God-given purpose. Sin is never polite; it is forceful.

Romans 7:15 says, "For what I do I allow not; for what I would, that do I not; but what I hate, that do I."

Here, Paul paints a perfect picture of the character of sin.

He is basically saying that sin left him powerless and without strength. He is showing us how sin seeks to control and rule our lives.

It is important to know that just like how Adam and Eve's choice caused the lives of others to come off course, it also only takes one decision to fall back in line with God, but it does not stop there.

As we live in Christ, we must continue to look at our lives and compare them to God's word to ensure they are lining up with the heart of God.

Looking at Genesis 4, we see that the two quickly moved on, beginning to have children who would grow and begin to make their own courses in life.

Moving on but never truly having the power to deal with what had occurred. Moving on to the "normal duties" of life.

Oftentimes, we find ourselves in that same position after something tragic or great occurs in our lives.

The only thing is that things are never really the same.

After a level of great heartbreak, trauma, pain, or loss, nothing would ever really be like what it once was.

No matter what, Adam and Eve couldn't go back to how things were in the Garden of Eden.

They could not turn back the hands of time to when they walked in the cool of the day and talked with God.

After a woman or a man is raped, they can never go back to how things used to be.

After a child sees his dad beat his mother, he is never the same.

What was once freedom and contentment that filled his heart was removed quickly replaced by fear, great concern and anger.

The little girl who comes face to face with her dad murdering her mother and then himself wears a scar that can't be washed away by bathing or covering up with any amount of makeup that she uses.

The wife who is forced to live with the shame of her husband's cheating ways is never the same no matter what she does. Every time he leaves to head to work, she finds herself wrapped in fear that her pain will never end.

The pastor who finds out that his son or daughter has a drug habit that has torn apart the family is never the same after he finds there is a habit that drives his once carefree child to chase a drug that only wants to breed death.

We get up, we wipe our faces, and we dust ourselves off and make a decision to press forward and continue.

Getting up and carrying on through life without truly facing what has happened.

Getting up and going to work every day. Working eight to ten hours all the while wearing a mask of perfection.

Raising children and never dealing with the root cause of what is wreaking havoc in your mind, heart, and emotions.

We are often found in church Sunday after Sunday wearing smiles and blending with the crowd all the while carrying secrets that are overwhelmingly heavy and unbearable.

We dance in church. We act as ushers. We are deacons. We are first ladies. We are singing in the choir. We are pastors. We are Sunday school teachers.

We are working close with the pastor; however, we find ourselves dealing with massive issues that remain covered up and left undealt with.

We are running large corporations. We are opening up businesses.

We are in school working to make life better for our families; however, if God were to shine a magnifying glass on our hearts, it would reveal brokenness, pain, and fear that has left us in a state of endless turmoil.

Gripped, controlled, and manipulated by fear and carrying on as if nothing has occurred.

Some have to take pills to get through the day and then find themselves taking pills to fall to sleep at night.

Some bound so tight that they can't make decisions from one moment to the next.

Some minister to many in church and then go home and face the brokenness that words can't even begin to describe.

Many fill the pews of church Sunday after Sunday and dancing or singing over pain but never really facing it.

Hurt, broken, and confused people who truly love God but feel trapped as if there is no way out.

Many are bound by memories of shame.

Dealing with depression and oppression, pretending all is well when some are broken and feel lost within their own minds.

Many have become nothing but great pretenders.

Some are even stuck in quoting the Bible off of memory and not off of their own personal experience.

Meaning without true connection to a certain Bible verse and just going through the motions to portray a certain image.

It is not God's desire that we fall into stating the word of God off of our memory. God wants us to have a fresh encounter with him that is life changing.

It is the fresh encounters with God that brings victories that change lives!

It is the fresh encounters with God that will turn lives around for the better.

It is the fresh encounters with God that will cause us to overcome and triumph even against the heaviest battles that rages against us.

Fresh encounters with God restore broken hearts, minds, and lives.

Fresh encounters with God uplift and propel a person to run toward their God-given purpose.

You see, it is good to be able to quote the word of God and to know the scripture word for word, but it is better to be connected to that scripture.

It is our personal experiences that connect us to God's word. Mama can know it, Daddy may know it, but when you know it, only then can it change you.

When we go from performing it to living it, then we'll see the true power of God begin to transform lives.

The body reacts to fear.

According to the California Science Center, this is how the body responds to fear:

First, the senses pick up that there is danger occurring or getting ready to occur. It does this through the eyes, ears, tongue, nose, and skin.

From here, a signal is quickly sent to the brain signaling there is possible trouble. Immediately following is a fight-or-flight response that begins.

Fear does not just stay in the mind; it also causes changes to take place within the human body. And this occurs very quickly.

The brain is very powerful and has the abilities to trigger past experiences where fear has occurred.

Next, we see something called the fight-or-flight stage, where the large organs such as the heart and lungs begin to work faster to keep up with what is occurring within the body.

With that being said, more oxygen is needed to keep up with the quick breathing. The heart will pump blood faster to muscles to help meet that need.

The nervous system, when it detects danger, causes the adrenal gland to release hormones such as adrenaline into the bloodstream.

From there, defensive behaviors are triggered.

Fear affects our skin because we quickly can start to perspire or sweat when we feel danger is near.

Fear causes extra blood to flow to large muscles such as our legs to prepare us for fight or flight.

So yes, fear takes over the natural body, and changes can be seen with the eyes.

Fear paralyzes.

Fear is known for the way it cripples and holds a person back from being truly who and what God has designed them to be.

The word of God makes it plain when it says in 2 Timothy 1:7, "For God has not given us a spirit of fear but of power, love and a strong mind."

There are the qualities God desires to fill our lives with. One can say that the Bible is the recipe for success in life.

Power to live, love that prevails, and a strong mind which helps to outlast all the wits, tricks, and assaults from the enemy of our souls is found in God's word.

Fear attacks these things: the body, the mind, the spirit, and eventually, the soul of a man. Let's look at these further.

1. The body. The body responds to fear by sweating, shaking, crying, screaming, anxiety, depression, and so on.

    Medical doctors have even stated that fear leads to many health issues. Here are a few: ulcers, strokes, heart attacks, stress attacks, mental breakdowns, anxiety which we have discussed briefly, migraines, and many more. All medical issues listed are all very serious.

    If you think Satan just comes to you without a well-thought-out plan when he drops fear at your feet, think again. Not only does he want you fearful but he aims to cripple and stop you from reaching the destiny God has in mind for you.

2. The mind. Fear is often described as "false evidence appearing real." This is because Satan works hard to get the mind of a man to see things totally opposite from what God does.

    God says you are free, and Satan wants you to see otherwise. God says, "I come that you might have peace," and Satan is saying you have no peace. God's word paints the picture of freedom, joy, and salvation. His word tells us who we are. God's word never sways from his promises.

From Genesis all the way to Revelation, we see an act of love pouring from the heart of God to man.

We see redeeming power that restores us from a fallen state of sin and positions us for greatness.

Satan works overtime to paint pictures of failure, lack, brokenness, and eternal damnation.

He paints pictures through the news that we see daily and pictures of devastation minute by minute.

Social media works as an avenue to tear down the image of God.

Satan pushes anger into our hearts by showing the racism, division, and pain.

There is a very real battle that occurs in the mind. It is one that only the word of God can gain victories in.

Powerful verses in the Bible such as 1 Corinthians 2:16 and Ephensians 4:23 say, "But we have the mind of Christ and Be renewed in the spirit of your mind. Both verses are life changing if applied during stressful situations."

It has been proven that where the mind goes, the body will soon follow. So it is a must that we gain victory in our minds before Satan does.

The word of God says in Philippians 4:8, "An idle mind it the devil's playground."

Which basically means that if you're not filling your mind with the word of God, it is filled with something else which will lead and control in a way that is contrary to the heart of God.

Meaning, if you're not in control, then someone else is.

God has given us tools in the word of God on how to have a mind of peace and joy.

FEAR SPEAKS

Fear has a voice that starts speaking right in the middle of trouble.

Fear comes on the scene in a way that puts people in a state of panic.

You could be going about your day, and then all of a sudden, fear has stepped on the scene.

You could be going about and handling business and here comes fear.

You could be in the middle of cleaning or right in the middle of traffic, and fear can show right up.

It could be anywhere. It could be at any time of the day.

You see, fear is different because it is not a friend you've welcomed.

Fear is not something you pencil into your calendar.

Fear is not something that you invite over for dinner or to the family barbecue.

No one is making room for fear in their home on purpose. No one is taking the time to move things out of the way in place of fear.

The key is to know that anytime fear is in a person's life, it is speaking.

Fear has a very contrasting nature to that of faith.

Fear is interruptive, never patient. Fear is paralyzing and never freeing.

Fear brings heartache, and it does not promote healing.

There is not another voice that compares to the voice of fear.

When fear opens its mouth and begins to speak, everything else stops.

Everything else is placed in a holding position when the voice of fear speaks.

You could be in a crowded room and all of a sudden be thrust into a private show where fear is on the stage performing in your heart, mind, or emotions.

Immediately, you're alone. Fear places a person in a dark and cold place. You see, fear can only bring discomfort.

So what is fear saying? Fear will boldly tell you how much of a failure you are.

Fear will proclaim why something could or would never work.

Fear says that you will never make it out of a current test or storm you're in the middle of.

Fear screams at the emotions and commands them to obey.

Fears pulls at the mind, making a case filled with doubt and pain.

The thing about fear is that its very intentions are to bring dread.

Dread that a loved one won't make it through depression and that suicide will be the phone call that you'll receive.

Some struggle with the fear of bad news.

Psalm 112:7 declares, "He shall not be afraid of bad news; his heart is fixed, trusting in the Lord."

Fear can have you expecting the heartache even though it has not occurred.

Dread of a broken heart even though a relationship is currently in a good place.

Dread of a son or a daughter getting caught up with wrong friends when at the moment everything is seemingly great.

Dread that you'll lose a home you have worked so hard to gain.

Dread that the cancer will return one day, causing life as you know it to crumble.

Dread that one day you'll get that thirst again for the bottle or pills that once controlled every waking moment of your life.

Dread that one day the happy family you have will fall apart and end up broken into more pieces than you can even begin to sort through.

Oh yes, you may try and portray perfection and act like you have complete control, but if fear is speaking in your life, then it is nothing but a performance.

SILENCING FEAR

If fear is speaking, than faith is not.

Fear must be silenced and be under control before faith can speak.

The Bible says in 2 Corinthians 10:5, "Casting down imaginations, and every high thing that exalteth itself against the knowledge of God, and bringing into captivity every thought to the obedience of Christ."

God is telling us to cast down the imaginations of fear. God is saying that you must take captive what is at work to bring you to captivity.

We see a state of action being required of us. Meaning, you can't just sit and allow fear to birth torment in your heart, mind, or emotions.

So how do we cast down fear? Simply by beginning to declare the word of God.

By deciding to speak faith over the fear in your heart, you quickly go from having no control to being in control.

Psalm 107:2 says, "Let the redeemed of the Lord say so, whom he has redeemed from the hand of the enemy."

We must speak up. Talk back to the fear that is at work to control and constantly have your life in an uproar.

Declaring the word of God is key when battling fear.

So take the word of God and find scriptures on who God says you are. And then every time that fear tries to rise up, throw the word of God back in its face.

Every time it attempts to remind you of that place of torment and shame, openly state the word of God.

I say the word of God is like medicine to the spirit, and every time you take it, it works victory through you.

It should be taken as often as can be. In whatever is trying to attack you, take the medicine.

In whatever is trying to throw you in dismay, take the medicine.

Take the medicine and expect results.

Take the medicine and expect change and turnaround.

Take the medicine and expect total victory over all that seeks to bring you down.

Now let's look at a few people in the Bible and see how they handled fear.

Saul's Fear of Losing the Kingdom

First Samuel 23 talks of how King Saul relentlessly pursued David throughout the land.

David was going out doing the business of God, and all Saul could think about was capturing David and his men.

Here in this text, you can see that Saul was pushed by his fear of losing the kingdom, fear of the kingdom falling into the hands of David.

Fear of all he knew slipping from his hands.

Fear has a way of driving a person and causing them to move on impulse.

Each time Saul heard that David and his men were near, Saul would drop everything to find them.

Saul would completely halt any and everything that he was doing in that moment.

Impulsive action is birthed out of fear.

You see in fear, there is no logic or thinking anything through.

Fear jumps. Fear jerks and fear pulls.

As you see, Saul awaited word on where David was.

Fear had him in a waiting position, and it caused him to look for a word.

A word that would tell him what his next steps would be.

Saul was not seeking God.

Saul was not praying so that he could be found on the path that God had chosen. No, Saul's focus was solely on David and his men.

Fear will rob a man of his focus.

Fear will rob a man of his concentration, and most importantly, fear will pull a person away from the original vision that was outlined for their life.

Instead of Saul pursuing the things that God desired, he turned and began to chase a man.

Fear pulled Saul off course. Fear put him in a position where he schemed and plotted day and night.

One contrast that you would see in this text is that David stood and prayed for God to give him direction. He stood on faith.

Saul stood on his fear and was motivated by it.

Here, we see a stance of faith and fear.

The two are drastically different. One would stop and wait for the voice of God, and the other does not seek direction.

One dropped everything in the moment carelessly, while the other remained busy doing the things of God.

Capturing David was all that Saul could see. His fear had blinded him. His fear had taken his peace and he found no rest.

Fear steals a person's peace, the peace that is able to sustain a person and hold through all he/she faces.

Fear brings an unsettledness with it when it comes to the scene. Saul had no rest.

The battle between fear and faith is more serious than we often see.

The way you respond to battle defines the life that you will live.

The lifestyles of fear and faith are like oil and water. You can't have both and walk in the victory that God desires.

As you maneuver through life, take a moment and see what is driving you.

Ask yourself, am I being driven by faith or fear?

Both have very different destinations and end results.

Moses's Fear of Not Being Good Enough

How often has God given you a task or placed a calling in your life that left you questioning your ability to perform or master it?

Have you ever been selected for a task that seemed to be too big for you or one that took you out of your comfort zone?

Moses found himself in this very place, a place where he felt the calling superseded his ability to fulfill the calling God had given him.

Moses heard all that God wanted and was then quickly reminded of his character flaws and personal issues.

There are two sides to every coin: There is the front, which shows great presence, character, and strength. Then there is the back of the coin that reveals what is not seen on the front of the coin.

Sometimes, all we see when God calls us is what makes us less or unworthy.

We see all the reasons why God has missed it in the selection process.

We see why it won't work and why we will fail at the task.

Moses's words to God were found in Exodus 4:10: "O my Lord I am not eloquent....but I am slow of speech and of a slow tongue."

How many times have you tried to convince God that he had it all wrong in the calling placed upon your life?

Moses thought it was important to remind God—the creator of the universe, the Lord of Lords—that he was not capable.

Moses thought it was needful to make sure God knew why he was not the man for the job.

Have you ever talked yourself out of being blessed or receiving what God had in store for you because all you could see were flaws within you?

How many times has God looked at you and told you that you were able and well equipped and you quickly reminded him differently?

God is saying you can do it or surpass a certain task and you raise your hand and say, "But, God, let me tell you why this won't work."

God is saying this is who I have called you to be and this is what you will do, but you raise your hand and say, "But, God."

Most of the time we focus on why something will fail instead of looking at why it can and will work.

Moses was focusing on the back of the coin of who he was.

Most of the time we dwell on the backside of the coin, but God sees the very best that he has placed within us.

Don't get so wrapped up in the backside of the coin that you miss the greatest miracles and blessings God has for you.

The backside has a way of stealing the shine that rests upon the best that God has in store.

The backside has a way of pulling you into a private show with your failures and mistakes on display.

The backside will continually tell you that you'll always be this broken person seeking a way out.

The backside will run your life if you let it.

The backside will hold you captive from advancing and growing.

It will tie you down with doubt and more questions than you can ever answer. It will blind you from seeing things as God sees it.

It will cause you to nurse your pain and never allow you to reach the promise God has outlined.

God wants us to come from the backside and get to the front of a thing. He wants us to be able to see what he sees.

Seeing it as God sees it can be tough if all you've seen for the majority of your life is failure and pain.

Seeing it as God sees it will mean that you have to let go of what causes you to view yourself less and not good enough.

Seeing as God sees will mean that you walk away from anything that is contrary to the vision God has of you.

You can take one picture and put it in front of two different people and both will see two very different pictures.

Oftentimes, what and how we see is tainted by our experiences and backgrounds.

Because that is the case, we often have to allow God to peel back the painful layers of our lives.

Peeling off the layers of pain and shame. Peeling off the layers of heartache and abuse.

It is important to know that every layer tells a story and paints a picture of why we are the way we are.

Instead of judging a person, stop and look at the layers that make up their lives.

Instead of turning your nose down on a person, stop and look at the layers that have shaped and formed the pains they carry daily.

Layer upon layer can reveal why a person is how they are.

Each layer as it is dealt with, can provide answers needed to some of life's greatest heartaches.

The homeless family that sleeps in a car has layers that tell a story that will cause even the strongest person to cry.

The drug addict who seems so out of reach has layers that can tell a story of abuse, neglect, and brokenness.

The overeater has layers upon layers that offer the key to why their life has quickly spiraled out of control.

The brokenhearted has layers upon layers where they have been let down and consumed by broken promises from those closest to them.

Even seemingly perfect families come with layers so deep that if an outsider looked just a little while longer, they would notice that something is just a little bit off and there is more than what they see.

Overachievers come with layers of the desire to please someone close to them. Most of the time, the overachiever is driven by the desire to be wanted, celebrated, and loved.

What are the layers of your life saying?

What are the layers of your life driving you to do?

Who are the layers of your life pushing you to be?

You see, we can grow up, we can move, we can change jobs, but until we deal with the layers of life, we'll never have complete victory.

You may smile and try to cover the pain up, but your layers will speak out.

You may try to cover it up with your money and the possessions that you have, but your layers are speaking.

Maybe you're a grown man or woman making your own decisions, but your layers reveal that you're that same little boy or girl stuck in a time that rendered you powerless.

Still that little boy who cries himself to sleep when thoughts of yesterday arise. Still that same little girl who shakes and trembles when she makes a choice that goes against the desires of her parents.

Trapped and stuck in a time where pain is an everyday occurrence.

Bound in a moment where you were taken advantage of with no strength to fight.

So instead of talking about where we are today or how far we have gone in life, let's focus on the layers that we carry daily.

You see, even if you move forward, make more money, or travel the world, layers left undealt with will always resurface.

We may brag about our pay grade. We gladly state where we live or how big our home is.

We talk about how our children are doing in school.

We'll even state our titles in church, but no one is standing up screaming, "I was raped when I was three and I am angry."

No one is shouting in church that "I hate my life and often think of ways to die."

No one is shouting on the mountaintop that "I can't get a grip on my life and I feel overwhelmed."

No one is proudly stating, "I am hurting and don't know what to do with my pain."

No one is saying, "I can't wait for my family to fall asleep at night so that I can finally cry myself to sleep."

No one is bragging about the layers that they carry.

But it is the layers that God wants.

When will we deal with the layers?

When will we get real with everything that plagues us daily?

When we will allow God to shine a light on the brokenness that resides within?

When we will discuss the elephant in the room?

God wants us to deal with all that is at work to pull us away from our purpose.

Take them to God and watch him work and bring victory.

Exodus 4:12 says, "Now therefore go, and I will be with thy mouth, and teach thee what thou should say."

Confession is powerful! The Bible tells us in Proverbs 18:21, "Death and life are in the power of the tongue, and those who love it will eat its fruits."

If you find yourself not knowing what to say or how to conquer a situation, start speaking God's word.

Exodus 4:12 makes it plain that God will teach you what to say. Sometimes, life's issues can leave us dumbfounded or at a loss for words.

God always reminds us that we're not alone and that he will be with us every step of the way.

You see, if the calling seems too big for you to accomplish, then you're right where you need to be.

Because it takes faith to believe in greatness even when all you can see are reasons why you'll fail at the task.

It takes faith for you to see yourself as what God has called you.

There will be times when you'll hear God say that you're strong in a moment where all you feel is weakness.

There will also be times in life when you'll hear God saying that you're able to gain victory but all you see when you look at your life are failure and brokenness.

You may feel too inadequate to succeed.

You may even feel like God got it wrong and should use another.

All Moses could see was his stutter. He couldn't get beyond the stutter.

The stutter was the thing that made him feel less or unworthy.

God is able to take that very thing that makes you feel less or unworthy and use it for his glory.

God is not second-guessing the calling upon your life just because of those inadequacies in your life.

God doesn't select a person because they're perfect.

All he needs is a willing vessel. One that will follow him as he works out all the kinks they have.

God looks for those who will go and walk out the calling placed upon them.

Can you get past your stutter? Can you get past the very thing that seems to count you out from the selection process?

What is it that makes you feel less or unworthy to be used by the God of the universe?

What is it that tells you you're not good enough to go and represent him?

What is it that you don't want people to know about you? What is the backside of the coin in your life?

Are there things in your past that pull you down from rising up every time God calls you?

Is there something in how you walk, talk, or carry yourself that holds you from moving ahead where God is calling you?

What is your stutter? It is important that you acknowledge the stutter in your life.

Acknowledge the issue.

Acknowledge the thing that threatens your growth and progress.

Acknowledge the thing that wants to hold you from advancing beyond where you are today.

Acknowledge the thing that wants to stop you from fulfilling the calling.

You see, God wanted Moses to know that his stutter did not disqualify him from mastering the calling upon his life.

The same for you, your stutter will not disqualify you from walking out the calling upon your life.

The very pain or stutter that you attempt to hide is the very thing that will bring you into a victory that you've never seen.

God desires to take that pain and bring you into a state of healing and complete soundness.

God takes us from pain to the promise when he starts speaking.

When you allow the word of God to speak over you, at that point you are moving from a state of loss to gain.

You see, there is power in the word of God and the Bible tells us that we can overcome by the blood of the lamb and our testimony.

Let's look at this Bible verse, Revelation 12:11: "And they overcame him by the blood of the lamb, and by the word of their testimony; and they loved not their lives unto the death."

So it is the blood of the lamb first and foremost that gives us access to victory.

Hebrews 9:12 says, "But by his own blood he entered in once into the holy place, having obtained eternal redemption for us."

So it is the blood of Jesus that has given us access and has granted us the authority needed to deal with all forms of fear.

The next part states by the word of their testimony.

So never be ashamed of your testimony. There is power in your story.

There is a strength that rises up in you when you tell your testimony.

Never be ashamed of your war wounds that you have obtained from the experiences you've faced. The world needs your war wounds.

The world needs your scars. What have you gone through?

What is it that you overcame that sought to bring you to ruin?

There is power in your testimony, and the gates of hell can't stop you from going forth when you realize this power.

Satan fights us and wants us to never know the power of our testimony.

He tells you that you should be ashamed, that you can't make a difference.

That you're the only one dealing with this area.

He will beat you with fear and attempt to highjack the promises that God has given you.

Know that when you speak, things begin to happen.

Demons get leery when you tell your testimony because the devil knows that the more you share the more strength you gain.

When you start to share your testimony, people will be set free because they see how God has turned things for you.

You see, as much as we want to cover things up and hide our pains, other people need them.

If your testimony touches one life, you have done a great work. Sharing a testimony builds faith within your heart

God wants us all to get past our stutter, to get past what makes you feel like a failure, to get past what causes you to feel unworthy in meeting the calling placed upon you.

Don't get stuck in the stutter. The area that causes you question or doubt who you are, don't get stuck there.

The devil would have it that you get stuck and never grow or produce greatness. But God says get up, there is more to come.

God is saying, "Come on, I have more waiting for you." God is saying, "I have victories for you ahead. Don't get stuck."

Oftentimes, a stutterer's greatest fear is public speaking and getting stuck on certain words, phrases, and not being able to move on.

The fear of people seeing them at their most vulnerable state. Fear of people seeing the backside of the coin in their lives.

Fear of people seeing them struggle and fight in an area they've had to fight in for the most part of their lives.

Moses was complete, and God could've used his stutter for his Glory.

God could've taken what seemed broken to Moses and brought a victory that was so amazing to where it inspired and lifted many, but because Moses couldn't get past his stutter and see God working, God had to use his brother Aaron.

God can use another to speak and work through whatever feels like the weakest part of your life, but he'd rather use you.

The beauty of it all is that even though Moses couldn't see past the stutter, God could.

Whatever you struggle with and fight with, God is able to use you for his Glory. Let him use your stutter.

Hezekiah's Fear of His Enemy's Words

Second Kings 18 and 19 tell the events of King Hezekiah. It starts off with all the great things that he did to clean up the kingdom.

We are shown a man of great strength and fortitude whose reliance is built on doing what is right in the eyes of God.

The same king who is seen bringing structure back to the kingdom and cleaning up all that was wrong in the kingdom is the same man whom we see down in 2 Kings 19 at the beginning of the chapter who is so distraught and worried that he tears his clothes after hearing the desires of his enemy.

Have you ever been so worried over what the enemy has stated that it shook you to your core?

You see, we often go from flowing and moving as God desires and then finding ourselves trapped in a place of fear over the words of our enemies.

Hezekiah was a king, so all the safety of his people rested upon his shoulders.

Although he had done great things and performed much for the advancement of his people, he still found himself in a position where fear had gripped him.

It is very easy to find yourself on the mountaintop one moment and then be in the lowest of valleys because of what is threating to pull you to a place of ruin.

Hezekiah heard what the enemy desired and it shook him.

He was shaken. He was greatly concerned.

This enemy was not one who only had a few victories under his belt. This was not one who just stumbled upon winning a battle here and there.

This was an enemy who was well trained and who had taken down other kingdoms.

The enemy even becomes bold and names all of his conquests and throws in Hezekiah's face the fact that he would be next.

The voice of the enemy is a calculated voice. It is a voice that comes to tear you from the place of rest that you have in God.

The voice of this enemy was very boastful and driven at bringing the king to his knees.

What is it that the enemy has spoken to you that has brought you to your knees?

What has the enemy stated that quickly took you from a place of great faith to one of great fear? What is your enemy saying?

You see, until a person deals with the voice of the enemy in their lives, they can never truly move to a place of victory.

Until you face what is trying to tear you down, you'll never truly walk in the purpose that God has placed in your life.

Face your enemy and deal with his words that he is hurling your way. Counteract the enemy's words with the word of God.

One thing that all enemies have in common is that they all bring fear with them when they come to the scene.

Cancer, HIV, diabetes, heart attack, terminal illness, depression, drugs, low self-esteem, failed marriages, every broken home, financial trouble and all forms of sexual perversions — they all have a fear that speaks.

But out of all of this, it is important to remember that God's word is a weapon. And once it is used, it can combat any fear that attempts to speak over you.

When your fear screams within and forces you to give in, find rest in the word of God.

In 2 Kings 19:6, we see the prophet Isaiah speaking: "Thus saith the Lord, be not afraid of what you have heard."

You see, God knows the enemy's words can shake us or make us afraid.

He knows that the threats can place worry and great concern in your heart.

But he reminded us here in this verse to not allow what we hear to place us into total panic.

Be not afraid of the medical report, of the news you just heard of that wayward son or daughter, of the depression that has come to swallow you up, of the current status of your marriage or of the devastation that you find running rampant in your life at this moment.

Someone may say, "Well, how can you say that?"

How can you tell me not to be fearful with all I am facing right at this moment in my life?

Maybe someone finds themselves facing a very strong enemy.

Someone may be dealing with a loved one who lies in his/her deathbed.

Someone else may be dealing with so much heartbreak that it is very tough to even utter how they feel at the moment.

Well God says, "Be not afraid." Be not afraid, knowing that he is with you.

Be not afraid knowing that this battle that you currently find yourself in is the Lord's.

Be not afraid knowing that God is skilled and knows just what is needed to gain victory over the enemy that wants to ruin you.

God never said or stated that Hezekiah had no reason not to fear.

God knows that we are human and live in a human body.

He knows that every now and again, we will face things that scare us to our very core.

He knows that the report from the medical exam you just took had shaken you.

He knows that you're very concerned for that loved one who has chosen drugs over their children.

He knows that you're fearful of getting a phone call that could utterly turn your world upside down.

The Bible tells us in Hebrews 4:15, "For we have not an high priest which cannot be touched with the feeling of our infirmities."

This means that God knows exactly how the situation you find yourself in is making you feel.

He is touched with our feelings and our very real emotions.

The walk of faith is one that is not controlled or ruled by our five senses.

It is a walk that holds dear to the word of God.

The Bible tells us in Hebrew 10:38 that the just shall live be his faith. It doesn't say that the just shall live by his feelings or emotions.

It doesn't tell us that the just shall live or be sustained by the current moment. It never says the just shall, "Live by the words of others."

It never says the just shall live by the current economic standing of the world around them.

It says, "The just shall live by faith."

That tells me that sometimes I will have to check my feelings at the door.

That means that I will have to defy my emotions and not give in to how they pull me here and there.

It means that I can be held in a position of faith even when my flesh speaks.

To be held by God when the enemy of fear seems to stand tallest in my life.

Faith that wraps me and grips me tighter than what has come to destroy me.

Faith that utters the words of God in my spirit even when I can't speak or move my lips.

Faith that rises even in the midst of total chaos.

You see, it is very true that if you build it, it will stand.

If you pour in words of faith, it will stand up in you right when you need it most.

Taking time to lay before God and soak in his word yields great benefits.

Put the word of God in so that when you need it most, it will show itself strong.

It is very important to store the word of God in your heart. David even said in Psalm 119:11, "Thy word have I hid in mine heart, that I might not sin against thee."

To hide the word of God in your heart is simply storing the word intentionally.

We will all have many ups and downs, but hiding God's word is a must. If we are to stand in great adversity, the word must be hidden.

If we're to rise from the broken places of our lives, the word of God must be hidden.

If we are to gain total victory over the enemy that comes to tear our family at the seams, the word of God must be hidden.

Hidden so deep that one bad day can't rip it out.

Hidden so far down to where the enemy can't reach in and rip it out.

Hidden past the surface and in the deep areas of our spirits to the point that it can't be found by the enemy of our lives.

David said, "Thy word have I hidden." This means that this is something David did. You see, David knew that his life would bring challenges.

You must also know that with life comes great challenge and you'll have need of intentionally hiding God's word within.

We must go from the state of offense to a state of defense.

We must get to a place where we're no longer standing and waiting for the storm to start and begin storing up the words of God within us.

There are those who only prepare for battles when the battles come, but God is saying that we must prepare and store well in advance.

Store up the word of God in your heart now so that when adversity comes, you are ready to stand against it.

Are you ready to stand?

Are you busy waiting and standing still, or are you in a storing position?

It's time to store up the words of God. It's time to be like the ant and prepare.

Be ready, get in position, for the Bible says, "That enemy walketh to and fro seeking who he may devour." The enemy walks to and fro seeking, which means he is busy looking and waiting for us to fail.

He is busy looking for a way in. He is busy and is moving.

So with that being said, do what you need to do to find yourself in a place of victory.

Do you need to be praying more? Then do it.

Do you need to go on a fast? Then do that.

Do you feel God working to pull you from a place of complacency?

Do you hear God calling you to go to a deeper level in him? Do you feel a tug to go higher?

Can you hear God calling you out of your stupor?

Whatever you need to do, do it.

Move in a way that will cause you to get right where God is drawing you.

You see, even though we may take a day off here and there, the enemy of our souls never rest. He is constantly moving and trying to pull us down.

He works in a way that lets us see the urgency of the times we live in.

He knows the moment he pulls back, it could cost him the victory.

He knows that if he pulls back from trying to bring you to ruin, you may advance far above his reach.

That is just what happens when you began to store up the word of God; it places you out of the reach of the enemy.

Out of reach to where he can't control or manipulate your life.

You see, there is power in the word of God, and this is why the battle is so great to get into the word of God.

There is a battle just to remain consistent in laying up the word in the heart of a man.

The battle comes because of the great victory that lies within the guidelines of God's word.

You see, within the word of God comes such a freedom that can't always be explained.

Within the deep places of God is a source of life that the enemy can't stand against.

When you get in the word of God, you gain the upper hand over the enemy.

You gain the upper hand over the habit that wants to crush you.

You take power over the shame that wants to control and hold you captive when you get in the word of God.

When you get in the word of God, lust has to bow down.

When you get in the word of God, that frustration has to move.

When you start to lay down before God, the grip that the enemy has over you has to move.

Do you know that in the word of God are the treasures and tools for living a victorious life?

The Bible says in Matthew 16:19, "And I will give unto thee the keys of the kingdom of heaven."

This means that God has given you the tools that allows you to live and walk in a way that God gets the glory in your life.

God wants to get the glory over that situation that has come to cripple you.

God wants to get the glory over the enemy that has been sent to destroy your family.

God wants you to gain the upper hand over the secret habit that you struggle with daily.

God wants to get the glory over the sickness that rises up every time you start to advance.

God wants the glory over the generations of issues that have plagued your family for many years.

God gets the glory every time we yield our lives to him.

Give it to him. You can't fix it anyway.

Give him the broken pieces of your family.

Give him the painful past you've tried to hide.

Give him the emotions that seem to be all over the place.

Give him the memories that have wounded you so to the point that you can't move forward.

Give him the shameful acts that you cover daily hoping no one would see. Give him the words that you replay over and over in your mind.

Give him the anger that you carry. Give him the you that no one has ever seen. Give it to him!

There is freedom when you give it to him.

There is liberty once you come to God and admit that you've lost control.

There is a victory that rises when you acknowledge that the burden has become too heavy.

There is a great peace that can start to flow when you tell God that you need him and can't go another step without him.

There is a joy that can move into your heart when you decide to let it go and give it all over to God.

You see, when we try to carry it or solve it, then there is such a bondage that comes.

When you pretend that all is under control, God can't move.

God can't move when you wear the mask that placed you in a holding pattern when you attempt to fix it or change it.

What Is My Faith Saying?

Faith says that I believe God enough to let it go.

Faith says that I take my hands off of it and release it to my God who is able.

Faith says that letting go is strength, and it leads me to untold victories.

Faith says that I realize I am not able to fix or change it and have a need of a God who can.

Faith puts me in a position of trust and reliance on God.

Faith moves me from the uncertain stance that my flesh has placed me in.

Faith changes the game. Faith flips the script of the enemy.

Faith places me on level ground.

Faith removes the stigma that the enemy has attempted to scar my life with.

Faith removes the control that the enemy has over me.

Faith tells me that I can, even when the enemy screams differently.

Faith reminds me of who God has called me to be.

Faith takes me from the losing side and places me on the grounds of victory.

Faith speaks over the voice of doubt, fear, and despair.

Faith builds me when I feel broken beyond restoration.

Faith takes back all that was stolen from me.

Faith gives me confidence to stand even when I am suffering.

Faith stores up life for me when death is everywhere I turn in this world.

Faith propels me forward even though complacency desires to hold me back.

Faith lifts me up when I have fallen.

Faith molds and reshapes my thoughts.

Faith directs me when I do not know where to go next.

Faith is my direction in a world of chaos.

Just like fear has a voice, so does faith and faith has the power to speak over your situation.

And Fear Crept In

Doors serve two sole purposes in homes, businesses, and building structures—to allow an entrance and an exit. Doors also serve as a protection mechanism.

They keep the wrong people, situations, and things out while also keeping the right people, situations, and things in.

There is a twofold process happening at the same time with the structure of the door.

Recently, I had an experience where there was an unlocked door at my home. I'm not sure how long in the course of the day was the door unlocked. But I do know that night came and the door was still unlocked.

I was not aware that the door was unlocked until I saw a man standing in the back of my house. At that time, it was too late to even begin to reason why, how, or who had left the door unlocked. All I could think of was, what now, Lord?

In that moment, I felt most vulnerable. I remember feeling out of my element like this was something I'd never encountered.

There was a man who I did not know standing in my home. The one good thing was that there was another door standing between him and me.

This door had a glass on it. So I could look out and he could see inside, but still, I was very scared and beyond fearful.

That moment, so many questions ran through my mind. How would I protect myself? What if these were my last moments? Would I live to tell the tale?

How would I protect the rest of my family inside the house, unaware of what was taking place? The biggest question was, Lord, how are you going to get me out of this situation?

It turned out that the guy was supposed to be next door at my neighbor's house. He left as quickly as he came in. I pointed him to the right direction, and he was off and on his way.

Closing the door and then leaning on it while taking a deep breath, I remembered I'd never been more relieved.

I was ever grateful that God had been with me during the interaction with the unknown man. I remember trying to sleep that night. I was very uneasy the entire night.

I was tossing and turning until my husband got home from work. As I began to restate what had occurred, I noticed that in that moment, fear had crept in. I was more than scared; I was horrified.

My heart was racing and my palms were sweaty even after a few days had passed. I began to tell God by the third day that I was scared. I began to quote scriptures focused on overcoming fear.

Second Timothy 1:7 says, "For God hath not given us the spirt of fear; but of power, and of love, and of a sound mind." And again, quoting it, "For God hath not given us the spirit of fear; but of power, and of love, and of a sound mind." And a day later I started saying, "For God hath not given me Natasha the spirit of fear; but of power, and of love, and of a sound mind."

I placed my name in the scripture and began to declare this over me each time fear rose up.

The more I quoted God's word, the bolder I became. The more I quoted God's word, the taller I stood against fear.

The word of God builds us up when we're most shaken. It calms our hearts when the world has run in like a flood.

God's word spoke for me when I had no voice against fear.

My attacker in that moment were the thoughts that endlessly filled my mind of what ifs. "What if this or what if that? Oh, and Lord, what about this?"

That moment taught me that the word of God can speak up even when you have been shaken.

The word of God can be your voice over the fear that tries to plague your life.

The word of God was my voice in moments where fear shook me to the cores of my soul.

In that moment, I understood how fear could creep in.

I understood firsthand how peace could quickly transform to torment and unrest.

God began to reveal to me that fear creeps in through doors of various experiences that we encounter in life.

Experiences that are not favorable. Experiences that are scary and painful.

God began to say that fear always has a door that it enters through. In life, there are various doors that can cause fear to move in.

A broken heart opens a door to fear. A broken relationship or a broken trust causes fear to enter.

Rape or sexual abuse can create fears that are often unexplainable to the victim. A divorce or abandonment also allows fear to creep in.

Being taken advantage of ushers in fears of its own as well. Being lied to or misled causes various fears to arise.

Dealing with illnesses or an untimely death can also be a door that fear enters in.

Being in the wrong place at the wrong time and seeing an act of violence have a whole harvest of fears that can come and manifest in more ways than a person can count.

You see, there are a million and one ways that fear can creep in and begin to take over a person's life.

One thing I noticed was that I kept reasoning with myself, saying, "What is wrong? Why am I so fearful?" I would say in the next moment, "I just had so much peace a moment ago, and now look."

God begins to tell that this is how quickly fear can move in. Have you ever been in a moment of great peace and calmness and then all of a sudden in a battle with fear?

Have things ever been flying high and then you find yourself crashing and trying to figure out why?

In that moment, you are in the battle of your life with fear being the opponent. Fear, your Goliath that needs to be conquered and brought down.

Sometimes, the giant seems taller and stronger than you can last remember yourself being. His muscles seem bigger and broader when he is standing before you.

Many people stare out and only see giants when they look at their life daily.

For some, giants come in the form of PTSD. Giants can come in the form of drug habits.

Giants may come in the form of uncontrolled eating or obesity. Some manifest in the form of sexual sins.

Giants may reveal themselves in competition with the ministry and in life as a whole.

Giants can arise in the form of failed marriages, failed churches, and seemingly failed lives.

Giants come on the scene in the form of mountain high debts.

Giants in the form of infertility. Giants come in the form of unmet expectations.

Giants that seem louder than the peace a person can carry.

Giants that seem to run faster and are stronger than the Bible verse you try to remember and call forth when needed.

Many men and women of God fight and struggle to maintain composure as they fight their way through various battles daily.

Fighting to maintain a smile when in front of people.

Walking out of church strongly and even boldly after a powerful Sunday service and wake only to fight a giant on Monday morning that appears unaffected and unmoved by the worship service one has just sat through.

Many are baffled and question what the key to gaining victory is.

Many lose sleep trying to figure out ways to outwit or gain the upper hand over an enemy they have fought for long periods of time.

Many even are fighting giants that seem to have gone from generation to generation in their families.

Fighting the giants of Grandma and Grandpa and even further back than that.

Many people are wrestling with heavy situations; and fear has seemingly gripped hearts, emotions, and souls.

The Bible states in John 10:10, "The thief comes only to steal and kill and destroy; I have come that they may have life, and have it to the full."

This tells us that Satan's direct motive is always the same—to steal, kill and eventually destroy.

Satan never switches up. He stays true to the same tactics: steal, kill, and destroy.

Seasons may change, but the goal is the same.

You may move from state to state, but the goal of Satan is unmoved.

You can change churches or homes, but the definite goal is still the same.

He wants to steal your faith, hope, joy, and strength.

He wants to kill your hopes and leave you in a state of total ruin.

He strives to destroy everything good that God seeks to birth within you.

Though we may slack off due to frustration, tiredness, or a heavy load of things to focus on, Satan never slacks off.

Well the Bible also tells us in 2 Peter 3:9, "The Lord is not slack concerning his promise, as some men count slackness."

So what he is saying here is that God is reminding us that he will not slack on his word or promise toward you or concerning the callings on your life.

He will not be slack on a good day or slack on a bad day. He remains faithful and consistent.

The faithfulness of God is revealed in the seasons that he has set in motion.

Genesis 8:22 declares that while the earth remains, seedtime and harvest, cold and heat, summer and winter, day and night shall not cease.

This is a word God declared way back in the beginning, and that word still yet stands firm.

Well just like the seasons and times of day, God's spoken word will prove sure and firm in your life.

You may feel like everything under your feet is crumbling and falling apart, but God's faithfulness will remain and that faith teaches us how to walk by faith even in the darkest times.

The key to comfort in any storm, test, or trial, the key is knowing that no matter what, God is there.

He teaches us what it really means to remain faithful in a faithless world.

He is the one constant in an ever-changing world. He is the very definition of what faith means.

He teaches us to stand by the very example of how he stood.

Thinking about the posture that Jesus maintained while walking this earth is overwhelmingly encouraging and uplifting.

And you may say, "Well I am not Jesus and you don't know my storm." You may feel beyond hopeless or broken beyond repair.

I want to remind you that the very nature of God rests on the inside.

When you took the leap and received Jesus in your heart, at that moment, the very nature of his presence moved in the very cores of your heart.

You may be saying, "Well, I am facing so much that I don't feel the presence of God at all in my situation." Or you may be saying, "I am so broken and I feel so low that I don't see myself coming out of this valley I am in."

But know that God is faithful and will make good on every single word he has spoken over your life.

The fact that you have breath running in your body proves his faithfulness.

You may have lost much and cried endless tears to fill the deepest ocean, but there is still purpose within you.

His faithfulness teaches us to stand when we feel like throwing up our hands and giving up.

Can you look in your life and still see the faithfulness of God even in the darkest moments of life?

Can you still look over the broken pieces and still find traces of his presence?

You may be saying that you don't know how to be faithful. Well, I challenge you: take a look at how each trying situation was handled when Jesus walked the earth.

Powerful Truths Found in God's Word

Yes, you'll go through moments where you feel there is no return, but remember the powerful truths found in the word of God.

Is Satan working? Yes!

Is he constantly seeking ways to bring you down and all you care about? Yes!

He works on your mind, emotions, and body.

He looks for an opening to come in and start to wreak havoc. He uses many avenues.

But the ending part of John 10:10 tells us that Jesus came that *we* may have life and have it to its fullest or in abundance.

That is the contrast to what the enemy gives. God is telling us that he is our hope and joy no matter what has risen against us.

I tell you today: no matter what or who your giant is, Jesus is standing and has already given you victory!

You're already the victor! Your fear may be the giant that you wrestle with, but God is your faith that will cause you to rise above it all.

You may be living in between fear and faith on a daily basis, but God is with you. You're never alone.

He promised he would never leave you nor forsake you, and he aims to keep his word!

Instead of rehearsing fears over and over, begin to call forth the powerful truths found in the word of God.

Too many times we get stuck in magnifying our pain and forget to magnify our God.

So when Satan starts to shake you by reminding you how painful life has been, begin to feed on God's truth.

Feed your faith and starve your doubts.

We feed our spirit each time we start to take the words of life.

Oftentimes, we are not eating enough. The way to stall the plans of the enemy is the cause and overflow of God's word.

Is the enemy hitting you at an overwhelming pace? Well, you hit back each time you find yourself in God's word.

Hit back! God's word puts you in position to fight back!

Are you in a fighting position?

You can only find endless victories if you're in a position combating against the tactics of the enemy of your souls.

So below, I have listed a few powerful truths that encourage and motivate my heart when the battle grows intense.

One of my favorite verses is found in Revelation 12:11. "And they overcame him by the blood of the Lamb, and by the word of their testimony; and they loved not their lives unto death."

It is by the blood of the Lamb of God that we are able to triumph any and all things that attempt to ruin our lives.

Hebrews 9:12 says, "He did not enter by the means of the blood of goats and calves; but he entered the Most Holy Place once and all by his own blood, thus obtaining eternal redemption."

Hebrews 9:13–14 tells us, "The blood of goats and bulls and the ashes of a heifer sprinkled on those who are ceremonially unclean sanctify them so that they are outwardly clean. How much more, then will the blood of Christ, who through the eternal Spirit offered himself unblemished to God, cleanse our consciences from acts that lead to death, so that we may serve the living God."

Glory to God! This tells us that God comes to cleanse us from the very acts that lead to death. Only God can come in and cleanse the heart, mind, and spirit from the acts of sin.

He cleanses and washes our conscience from the yoke that binds us to the very acts of the things we have done that pulled us from God.

Where sin separated and pulled, God came in with his blood and restored and mended us whole as if there was never a breakage.

There is power in the blood of Jesus! There is keeping power in the blood of Jesus. And when we stand in his name, he shields us when life rains down brokenness and pain that can't be explained.

When we call on the name of Jesus and stand in him, we become stronger and wiser than any giant that attempts to stand before us.

Matthew 17 tells a parable of a father who brought his son before the disciples, stating that his son was a lunatic and was vexed.

He went on to state that he would fall into fire and into water, and the father ended by saying the disciples could not cure him. Jesus moves in, rebukes the devil, and he departs out of the child, leaving the child free.

Let's look deeper at Matthew 17:21: "Howbeit this kind goeth not out but by prayer and fasting."

There are some things that require spending time in prayer and fasting for victory to come forth.

The greatest of giants can be conquered from times of prayer and fasting.

Take moments to intentionally set aside times of prayer followed by fasting.

In my time of salvation and dealing with struggles of life, I have come to see that the devil is very intentional in all he does.

He never gives a moment of fleeing gratification because he wants you happy.

He never makes you feel high on life because he wants the best for you.

He is intentional, calculated, and sorely focused.

With that being said, we as women and men of God have to be intentional with creating time for God.

We must steal away moments to lie down before the presence of God.

That can mean setting up days where you read the word of God, or if that means lying at his feet in worship after a long day, be intentional.

Declaring God's Word over Fear, Confessions of Triumph

God's word gives many scriptures the help to address and overcome fear.

The word of God is the source of strength when fear tries to get the upper hand in life.

Here are a few below that I hold dear and meditate on when needed.

1. "Say to those with fearful hearts, 'Be strong, and do not fear, for your God is coming to destroy your enemies. He is coming to save you'" (Isa. 35:4).

2. "I am leaving you with a gift, peace of mind and heart. And the peace I give is a gift the world cannot give. So don't be troubled or afraid" (John 14:27).

3. "This is my command, be strong and courageous! Do not be afraid or discouraged. For the Lord your God is with you wherever you go" (Josh. 1:9).

4. "So don't worry about tomorrow, for tomorrow will bring its own worries. Today's trouble is enough for today" (Matt. 6:34).

5. "Do not be afraid, for I have ransomed you. I have called you by name; you are mine" (Isa. 43:1).

6. "Even though I walk through the darkest valley, I will fear no evil, for you are with me" (Ps. 23:4).

7. "I prayed to the Lord, and he answered me. He freed me from all my fears" (Ps. 34:4).

8. "When doubts filled my mind, your comfort gave me renewed hope and cheer" (Ps. 94:19).

9. "Give all your worries and cares to God, for he cares about you" (1 Pet. 5:7).

10. "Do not be afraid of them; the Lord your God himself will fight for you" (Deut. 3:22).

11. "Do not be afraid of anyone, for judgment belongs to God" (Deut. 1:17).

12. "When I am afraid, I put my trust in you" (Ps. 56:3).

13. "He will cover you with his feathers. He will shelter you with his wings. His faithful promises are your armor and protection. Do not be afraid of the terrors of the night, nor the arrow that flies in the day. Do not dread the disease that stalks in darkness, nor the disaster that strikes at midday. Though a thousand fall at your side, though ten thousand are dying around you, these evils will not touch you" (Ps. 91:4–8).

14. "I, am the one who comforts you. So why are you afraid of mere humans, who wither like the grass and disappear" (Isa. 51:12).
15. "Be not afraid of them {their faces}, for I am with you to deliver you, says the Lord" (Jer. 1:8).
16. "Fear not; you will no longer live in shame. Don't be afraid; there is no more disgrace for you" (Isa. 54:4).
17. "We have been rescued from our enemies so we can serve God without fear, in holiness and righteousness for as long as we live" (Luke 1:74–75).
18. "Jesus told him, 'Don't be afraid; just believe'" (Mark 5:36).
19. "For God hath not given us the spirit of fear; but of power, and of love, and of a sound mind" (2 Tim. 1:7).

And lastly, my favorite:

20. "There is no fear in love; but perfect love casteth out fear: because fear hath torment. He that feareth is not made perfect in love" (1 John 4:18).

Get yourself a good Bible that can break down God's word for you.

If there is a version that you have trouble understanding, there are various versions to utilize.

I often find myself breaking down the scriptures by using a few different versions to continue my study.

What I mean is you should get what will work best for your understanding.

If you are hungry for God and you open up the word, you're guaranteed to find life and tactics for defeating what is fighting against you.

Even just by asking the Holy Spirit, he will lead you to the verses or verse needed for your current moment.

He has done it for me, and I know that he'll do the same for you.

Fear's Stance in the Word of God

It has been said that the phrase "Fear not" is listed in the Bible 365 times.

God's word equips us and empowers to live a fearless life daily.

Because of the many complexities of life, God's word is filled with all that we need to triumph.

As you go through life, take God's word with you. It is that same word that will hold and sustain you in the darkest moments of life.

Fear comes in many shapes and forms. But God's word is a constant and it will build fortitude and stability.

Though we face many valleys and mountains in life, the weapon of victory is found in the Bible.

Fear is the greatest weapon Satan uses to fight against the people of God.

It is important to run to the word of God and not from the word of God.

When you find yourself gripped or battling fear, pull out the word of God and start to declare the life found in it over you.

As you begin to speak the word, healing will start to flow over you. The healing you will find will begin to empower you and strengthen you against all that is fighting against you.

On somedays, you'll have to talk yourself through the pain, heartache, and brokenness of life.

It is said that a solider must never go to a battle or a war without weapons or being ill prepared.

All soldiers go with the mind-set of protecting themselves or fighting for a greater cause.

As a child of God, we will often face battles that seem unspeakable, but the weapon that will lead us to victory will always be the word of God.

Are you in a battle without the word of God?

Are you facing trials uncovered and ill prepared?

Never go out uncovered; take God's word.

You are a solider, and God's word is the covering that you need to stand tall as God designed.

The Bible tells us in Genesis 1:27 how man was created in his own image.

In the image of God, there is no fear.

Take a moment and think of the image of God and the power that rests in that image.

The image of God will reveal what should be in our lives.

When you face trials and various traumas, ask yourself, how does this line up with the image of God?

The fear that seeks to control you or bind you, is this in the image of God?

One thing that is known about fear is that it controls and causes a person to slowly conform to a life and mind-set of bondage.

Fear doesn't take control over a person's life all in one moment. There is a process that slowly occurs in a person's life.

But in the word of God, there is strength and overcoming power.

The real truth is that it doesn't happen overnight and you may not be free overnight from fear.

Because pain comes in layers and so do fear and healing.

Oftentimes, people think that if they join a church, all their fears and pains will quickly go away.

Or that if they just completely change their life, all their fears will go away.

But the truth is that even if a person joins a church, makes every service, or even changes their environment, if not dealt with or faced, the fears that plague will still remain.

Fear has to be addressed and can't be swept under a rug.

As a child of God, we must be constant in standing with the word.

Constant, intentional, and purposeful.

Address fear—do something!

Addressing fear is very important. Overcoming fear doesn't happen without taking active steps to do so.

The Bible tells us that faith without works is dead. Faith requires works for it to be fully effective.

Faith requires that action occurs. Faith is praying, but action is getting up and acting on the word of God that you have prayed on.

Faith is believing and maintaining confidence on the word, but action demands that you get up and do something.

A person can pray for finances needed for a certain task, but action is required to make it complete.

If that comes in the form of getting a new job, that is action.

A person can desire to clean up their credit, but they must begin to also make adjustments financially that will lead them in the direction of improvement of credit.

That will mean cutting back, budgeting, or going for financial counseling.

Oftentimes, a whole new mind-set is needed to proceed in a healthy direction.

Addressing fear can come in many ways.

The past has to be dealt with. The abused can't just wish the pain endured from their abuser away. It must be addressed.

A person who has been misled and taken advantage of doesn't wake up one morning and just willingly offer trust.

The brokenness in them must be dealt with and faced head on.

The church minster who has been overlooked and ignored doesn't walk away from the hurt overnight or sing the pain away. It must be addressed.

So you may not know what to do or what addressing it looks like for your situation.

Maybe you question what addressing it means for you.

Begin seeking God, and he will lead you to what is best for you. There is no one way to address or handle a situation.

God is able to give you just what you need to cause victory and freedom to break forth in you.

Here are just a few examples of what addressing it may look like for some.

Addressing it can come in the form of forgiving yourself or someone else.

Addressing it can come in the form of seeking medical attention.

Addressing it can come in the form of a therapy session.

Addressing it can come in the form of recognizing unhealthy environments or relationships and knowing when to move forward.

Addressing it can come in the form of speaking up for yourself.

Oftentimes, the captor's power is in what they say and how they craftily get in the mind of the victim. So here, talking back is very powerful!

Every time you speak out, you're building strength and fortitude over whatever is seeking to bring you into bondage.

Ask God to help you address it so that you can find the victory you need.

Ask God to show you how to gain victory over the fear in your life.

Tell God that you need him and that you can't do it without him.

Prayer is key. Combine prayer with reading and studying the word of God.

Also, surround yourself with people who will promote healing and not pain.

The people around us can either push us further in life or they can pull us back.

Who or what is pulling you? Are they leading you deeper into the abyss of fear or are they pulling you out of it?

Addressing it is a very pivotal key in overcoming fear.

THE PATH TOWARD HEALING

A person can never conquer what they have refused to address or face.

So if you're still covering it up or hiding the scars of it, then you will be dealing with it for a while.

Oftentimes, that means ripping the Band-Aid off and allowing the healing process to take its course.

Giving it room to breathe to see what the damage really is.

Look at the scars that the fear left and know that this too can be healed and overcome.

Ask God for boldness in gaining victory over the fear.

It may not be something that you have caused to come up on your life.

Most of the time, we don't take part in birthing the pain, but we can take a part in the healing process.

This is your opportunity to gain the upper hand in the next seasons of your life.

When you begin taking back your power, the enemy can no longer hold it over your head.

When the shame is gone from it, it has lost its power over you.

So I say this to tell you that you'll start to know you are on the path to healing when the shame of it is no longer there.

When you no longer hide from it, you're on the path to healing.

When you can speak the names of those who caused the brokenness within and even do so without having painful flashbacks, you're on the path toward healing.

When you can stand up and shake the dust off of you and start to see changes for the better in you, then you're on the path toward healing.

You see, we have to make it up in our mind to accept the healing process that God desires to begin.

You have to surrender to the plan of healing.

It is like a person who needs medical attention. The doctor may prescribe needed medicines or even better eating habits, but if we don't chose to totally surrender to the plans, healing will not fully come.

God is saying, "I want to bring healing where you need it most, but I need you to take part in the healing process as well. I need total surrender."

Some pains are so deep and so dreadful that only God can surgically handle.

You may have tried many things and found no healing from the fear that has plagued you.

You may have tried to fill the void in your heart with many different relationships.

You may even think the pills will work or alleviate the pains from your childhood.

You may think money is the answer and that by having the best of possessions will resolve it all.

Maybe you've tried surrounding yourself with people at all times to avoid being alone.

You may be waiting on the next opportunity, thinking that next big break will put you right where you need to be to get over what you have spent years getting over from.

Well, I am telling you that only Jesus can fill the void and begin the healing process within.

Name your fear, name the issue, and I tell you God has the word of victory just for you.

First Peter 2:11 says, "Dear friends, I warn you as temporary residents and foreigner's to keep away from worldly desires that wage against your very soul."

So with that being said, we are passing through. Is it possible to live in between faith and a world of fear and do so victoriously?

Yes! God's word gives the keys that will allow so.

The truth is we are in between faith and fear. The truth is that we overcome our greatest fears by leaning on the faith that comes from God's word.

Living in a world that has many fears and worries.

Living in a world that has many ups and may downs that we all sometimes experience in the same day.

In between, holding fast to God's word but also having to face defeat and unspeakable pains.

In between, the problem and the promise.

In between, joy but also facing severely discouraging moments that can break even the strongest.

In between, a mighty spoken word from God all the while enduring letdowns from those closest to us.

In between, the faith of it and staring fear right in the eyes in the same breath.

In between, the great gulf of God's word and the doubts Satan seeks to fill our minds with.

While we are in this world, there will be trauma and heartaches.

In our time on this earth, we will experience both good and bad.

There will be days when it only seems to rain on us.

Some days' rain storms of favor, blessings, and miracles.

While on this earth, the storm could be rains of loss, health scares, and even deaths of loved ones.

Ground zero is often what I call the faith walk. We are right in the thick of it.

Ground zero means being so close that you can feel both worlds.

Ground zero means that you are so close that you can reach out and grab both.

In between faith and fear.

Some days, it will seem one is moving or flowing more than the other.

Every day, our eyes open and we're graced with another moment of life we have a choice to make.

Faith or fear. What will you choose?

Will you pitch your tent on the side of fear or faith?

Will you allow fear to control you for the remainder of your days?

Will you get up and walk away from fear and grasp faith tightly?

It is true that while we exist in this body of flesh we will face fears, but it is also very true that we can decide to live a life a faith.

Abandoning fear is an active decision that only you can make.

Abandoning the thoughts of a lifestyle of fear.

Abandoning the habits that fear has brought into your daily life.

Abandoning the excuses made as to why fear is the easiest route to take.

Taking power back is a must if you're to experience victories from God.

Heaven's gift to you is true freedom.

Heaven's gift to you is undisturbed peace.

Heaven's gift to you is power over what threatens to take you under.

God tells us in Hebrews 12:1, "Therefore, since we are surrounded by such a great cloud of witnesses, let us throw off everything that hinders and the sin that so easily entangles. And let us run with perseverance the race marked out for us."

So here, the witnesses are those who are listed in the hall of fame in Hebrews 11. Basically, they are pushing for you to win the race. This is a cloud of witnesses who are well equipped with pain, heartache, loss, death, and much, much more.

Let's look at our witnesses: Abel, Enoch, Noah, Abraham, Isaac, Jacob, Sarah, Joseph, Moses, Rahab, Gideon, Barak, Samson, Jephthah, David, Samuel, the prophets, and many others.

This is known as the hallmark of faith because it lists out the struggles and trials of those in the Bible who refused to give up.

So when you feel weak or that you can't go a step further, this will inspire, uplift you.

You think you have gone through adversity? Look at some of their lives.

You see many sides of fear. You'll see determination. You'll find strength needed for tomorrow.

You see the well-known and those who lived lives on the unknown spectrum as well.

It takes time to break down highs and also very low lows.

Be encouraged knowing that God is not alarmed by what is attempting to kill out your destiny and purpose.

Know that God is not ashamed of you or has grown tired of you.

He is in your corner even if you have given up on yourself.

Begin to exchange your view for his and you too will begin to see that living victorious between faith and fear is a possibility.

Living between faith and fear is a daily walk.

God grants overcoming keys in his word.

So as you journey through this life, do just that—live.

You may be in between the two, but choose faith and live with the mind-set knowing that God has it all laid out for you.

Steps of purpose and triumph.

The word of God equips us to rise above it all. God causes us to victoriously succeed all the while living in between faith and fear.

ABOUT THE AUTHOR

Natasha Aughtry currently resides in Buffalo, NY, with her husband and two children. Her greatest passion is encouraging and motivating people to be the very best they can be in God and in life as a whole.

Serving at International Word of Faith Ministries where her pastors are Jeffery and Gwen Crawford, she works wherever needed to assist the ministry.

Natasha has been working in Ministry for over seventeen years and is driven and motivated by the heart of God.

CPSIA information can be obtained
at www.ICGtesting.com
Printed in the USA
LVHW090039230520
656338LV00007B/942